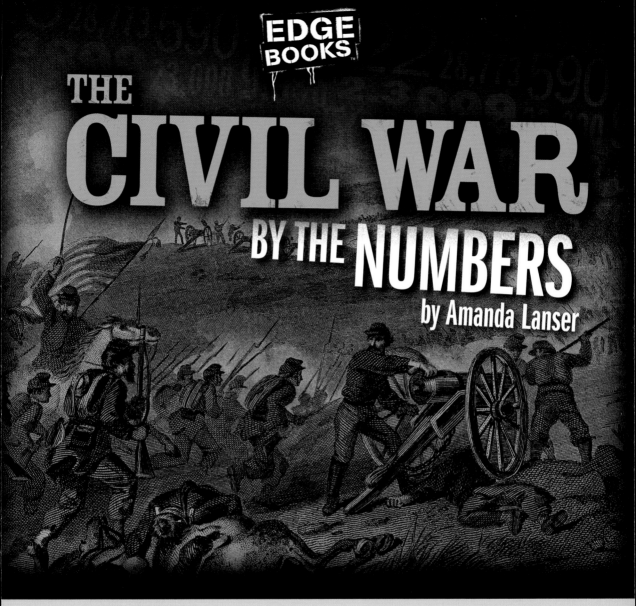

EDGE BOOKS

THE CIVIL WAR
BY THE NUMBERS

by Amanda Lanser

Consultant:

Barbara Gannon PhD

Assistant Professor, History

University of Central Florida

Orlando, Florida

CAPSTONE PRESS
a capstone imprint

Edge Books are published by Capstone Press,
1710 Roe Crest Drive, North Mankato, Minnesota 56003
www.capstonepub.com

Library of Congress Cataloging-in-Publication Data
Lanser, Amanda.
  The Civil War by the numbers / by Amanda Lanser.
      pages cm.—(Edge books. America at war by the numbers.)
  Summary: "Describes aspects of the U.S. Civil War using numbers, stats,
and infographics"—Provided by publisher.
  Includes bibliographical references and index.
  ISBN 978-1-4914-4295-1 (library binding)
  ISBN 978-1-4914-4331-6 (ebook pdf)
  1. United States—History—Civil War, 1861–1865—Juvenile literature. I. Title.
  E468.L26 2016
  973.7—dc23   2015000535

Editorial Credits
Arnold Ringstad, editor
Craig Hinton, designer
Jake Nordby, production specialist

Photo Credits
AP Images: 10–11, 17, National Archives and Records Administration, 21 (top), Paul Philippoteaux, cover (background), 1; Corbis:
20, Bettmann, 23, National Geographic Creative/Tom Lovell, 26–27; iStockphoto: duncan1890, 3 (right), pelicankate, 21 (bottom);
National Park Service: Antietam National Battlefield, Maryland/James Hope, 22 (top); Library of Congress: Print and Photographs
Division, cover (foreground), 8–9, 12–13, 16, 18–19, 28, Alexander Gardner, 29, Charles R. Rees, 10 (left), Octavius Carr Darley,
24–25, Julian B. Vannerson, 15 (bottom left), Kurz & Allison, 2, 14–15; North Wind Picture Archives, 6–7; Shutterstock: Audrey
Kuzmin, 21 (plaque), cheesekerbs, 25 (crop icons), Dan Thornberg, 22 (bottom), nazlisart, 3 (left), Ranier Lesniewski, 4–5 map, 12
(map), Rob Byron, 11 (top), Todd Taulman, 8 (left), Victoria Andreas, 21 (background, frame), Yoko Design, 25 (animal icons)

Design Elements
Red Line Editorial (infographics); Shutterstock Images: Ken Schulze (smoke), Picsfive (chains)

Printed in the United States of America in North Mankato, Minnesota.
042015   008823CGF15

Table of Contents

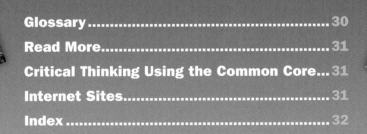

A UNION DIVIDED

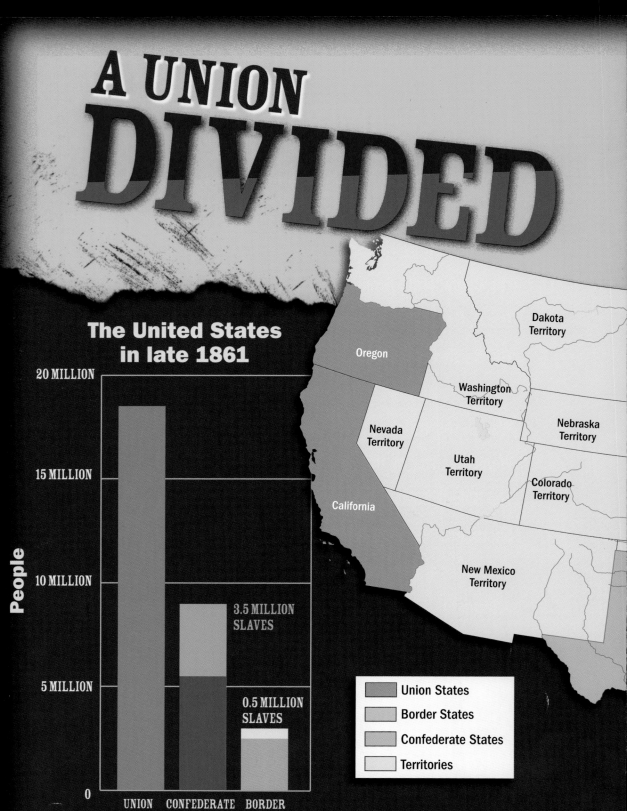

The United States in late 1861

People

- 20 MILLION
- 15 MILLION
- 10 MILLION
- 5 MILLION
- 0

UNION CONFEDERATE BORDER

3.5 MILLION SLAVES

0.5 MILLION SLAVES

Oregon

Washington Territory

Dakota Territory

Nebraska Territory

Nevada Territory

Utah Territory

Colorado Territory

California

New Mexico Territory

Union States
Border States
Confederate States
Territories

By the mid 1800s, Americans saw a bitter, violent struggle on the horizon. Many Southerners wanted to keep slavery legal. They believed states should decide for themselves whether slavery should be allowed. Many Northerners wanted to **abolish** the practice throughout the nation and stop it from spreading to new states. By the time Abraham Lincoln won the 1860 presidential election, the issue of slavery had divided the country. States began to **secede** from the United States in late 1860 and early 1861, forming the Confederate States of America. The stage was set for the Civil War. This is the war between the states—by the numbers.

19
Union states

5
border states

11
Confederate states

abolish—to get rid of something completely
secede—to leave a political group

SLAVERY

Southerners in 1860

67% non–African-Americans

33% African-Americans

African-Americans in 1860

11% Free

89% slaves

white U.S. families in 1860

75% owned no slaves

1% owned 40 or more slaves

24% owned 1–39 slaves

$800 average price of a slave in 1860; that translates to $20,000 today

3/5 amount of a whole person a slave was worth for tax and voting purposes. The ratio came from the Three-Fifths Compromise of 1787. The number of people in a state affected how many votes the state received in elections. It also affected how much the state had to pay in taxes. Southerners wanted more votes but wanted to pay fewer taxes. People in the North did not want slave owners to have a larger influence on elections. The result was the Three-Fifths Compromise.

56 people killed in Kansas over the issue of slavery between 1854 and 1861

1 white individual=1 person

1 slave= $\frac{3}{5}$ person

7 Southern states that seceded from the Union between Lincoln's election and the first battle of the Civil War at Fort Sumter

$1,000 AND 6 MONTHS JAIL TIME penalty for harboring or concealing a **fugitive** slave under the 1850 Fugitive Slave Act

U.S. population in 1860

87% total free population of the United States

13% total slave population of the United States

fugitive—a person who has escaped and is hiding from people who wish to capture or harm him or her

THE UNION ARMY

2,672,341 people who **enlisted** in the Union army

📇 = 100,000

Jobs of Union Soldiers

48% farmers

40% mechanics and laborers

9% other

3% professionals, such as lawyers and doctors

3,530 American Indians who served in the Union army

178,975 African-Americans who served in the Union army

enlisted—enrolled in the army or other branch of the military

2:1 ratio of Union soldiers to Confederate soldiers at the peak of the war in 1863

1.5 million horses used by the Union army

$13 monthly pay of a white Union private in 1863

amount taken from a white Union soldier's pay to cover the cost of his uniform **$0**

$10 monthly pay of an African-American Union private in 1863

amount taken from an African-American Union soldier's pay to cover the cost of his uniform **$3**

THE CONFEDERATE ARMY

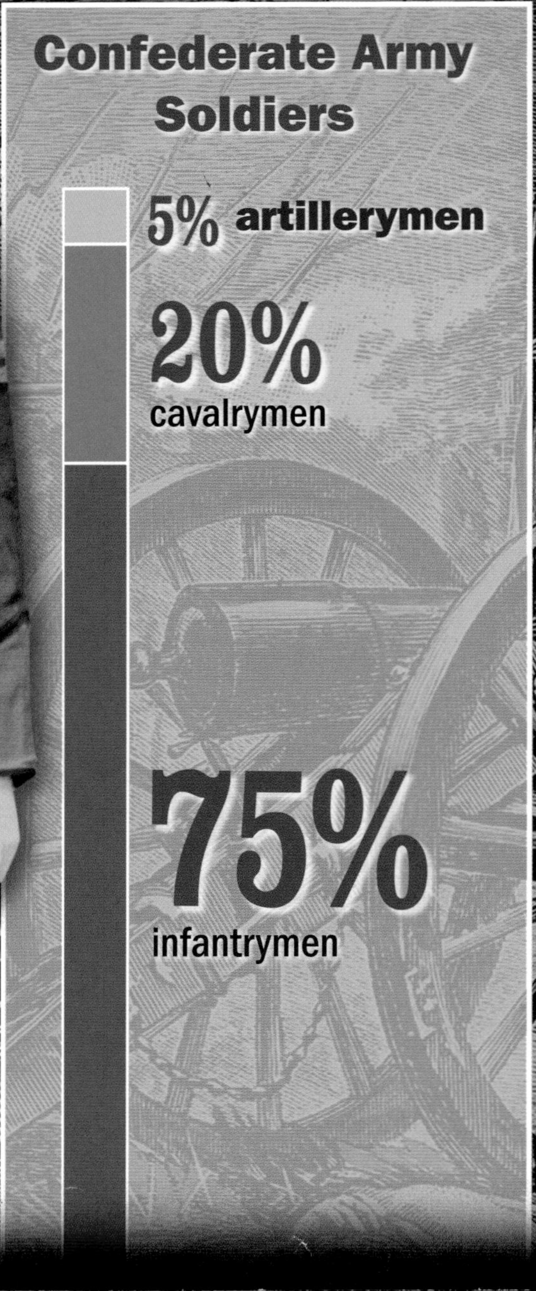

Confederate Army Soldiers

5% **artillerymen**

20% cavalrymen

75% infantrymen

artilleryman—a soldier who operates cannons or other large guns used during battles

18-35
the age range of the Confederate army's draft, passed in April 1862

17-50
the age range of the Confederate army's draft after February 1864, due to a lack of soldiers

600,000
rifles imported by the Confederacy from Europe

1.2 MILLION
approximate number of people who served in the Confederate army

 =100,000

3,000
approximate number of African-Americans who served in the Confederate army

1.5 million
horses used by the Confederate army

Jobs of Confederate Soldiers

15% other

2% professionals, such as lawyers and doctors

14% mechanics and laborers

69% farmers

THE BATTLE OF FORT SUMTER

The secession of South Carolina in late 1860 worried U.S. Army troops at Fort Sumter. The island fort was located in the harbor of Charleston, South Carolina. Attempts to resupply the fort were blocked by Confederate cannon fire from the shore. A month after President Lincoln's **inauguration** in March 1861, Confederate Brigadier General P.G.T. Beauregard demanded the surrender of the fort. When the U.S. Army refused, Beauregard ordered an attack. It was the first battle of the Civil War.

85 Union soldiers stationed at Fort Sumter when South Carolina seceded from the Union

6 WEEKS the amount of time the Union soldiers' supplies would last after Lincoln's inauguration

Virginia

North Carolina

South Carolina

Georgia

★ Fort Sumter

Florida

N W E S

4:20 a.m.

time on April 12, 1861, that
the Confederates started
their artillery attack

1861

APRIL 11

Confederate Brigadier General
P.G.T. Beauregard ordered the fort
to surrender, but Union commander
Major Robert Anderson refused

APRIL 12

APRIL 13

date the Union forces at Fort
Sumter agreed to surrender

34

hours the Confederate
attack on Fort Sumter lasted

0

casualties in the Battle of Fort Sumter

inauguration—a ceremony to place a new
president in office
casualty—a soldier who is dead, wounded,
missing, or captured after a battle

13

THE BATTLES OF
BULL RUN

Confederate and Union troops clashed in northern Virginia in the First Battle of Bull Run on July 21, 1861. It was the first major land battle of the Civil War. Union troops wanted to open a route to the Confederate capital of Richmond, Virginia. However, the fighting did not go in their favor. The Confederates blocked the Union from advancing and forced Union troops to retreat back to Washington, D.C.

Number of Soldiers in the First Battle of Bull Run

	0	5,000	10,000	15,000	20,000	25,000	30,000	35,000

in combat

killed

wounded

Union

Confederate

5:00 p.m.
time on July 21 the Union forces began their retreat to Washington, D.C.

30
average pounds of equipment an infantryman carried at the First Battle of Bull Run

skirmish—a minor fight between small groups of troops
flank—the side of a military formation

Confederate and Union troops met again at the Second Battle of Bull Run in August 1862. Union troops were organized there to defend Washington, D.C. After small **skirmishes** along the Rappahannock River, fighting began in earnest on August 28. The battle lasted three days and resulted in another Confederate victory.

Number of Soldiers in the Second Battle of Bull Run

	0	10,000	20,000	30,000	40,000	50,000	60,000	70,000	80,000
in combat									
killed									
wounded									

■ **Union**
■ **Confederate**

28,000
Confederate troops that attacked the Union **flank** at the same time. It was the largest single assault of the war.

2 the number of groups Confederate General Robert E. Lee split his forces into. One half attacked the Union troops directly. The other half attacked Union forces from the side, bringing about a Union defeat.

CONFEDERATE CITIES UNDER SIEGE

Most of the battles of the Civil War took place in the South. The Union army marched through Confederate territory. Rather than attacking cities, armies sometimes surrounded them, preventing supplies from getting in the cities. Then those laying **siege** would wait for the defenders to surrender.

Siege of Yorktown

APRIL 5–MAY 4, 1862 dates of the siege of Yorktown, Virginia

29 days the siege lasted

12 miles of new **fortifications** built by the Confederates in anticipation of the Union offensive

11,000 Confederate soldiers who retreated on May 4

101 other Union artillery pieces present at Yorktown

40 Union **mortars** present at Yorktown

siege—the act of surrounding a city and its inhabitants in hopes of capturing it
fortification—a structure used to defend a city
mortar—a cannon that fires bombs at high angles and at short ranges

16

Siege of Vicksburg

MAY 18–JULY 4, 1863 — dates of the siege of Vicksburg, Mississippi

47 — days the siege lasted

6,000 — population the city of Vicksburg was designed to hold

30,000 — Confederate troops stationed in Vicksburg during the siege

77,000 — Union troops who laid siege to Vicksburg

29,491 — Confederate troops who surrendered at Vicksburg on July 4, 1863

WAR ON THE

The Confederate Navy

0 ships in the Confederate navy in 1861

130 ships in the Confederate navy by 1865

8 crewmen aboard the Confederate submarine *H.L. Hunley* in history's first successful submarine attack in February 1864

5 months between the end of the Civil War and the surrender of the last Confederate ship, the CSS *Shenandoah*. It had been patrolling in the Pacific Ocean.

MARCH 8-9, 1862 dates of the first ironclad battle, which was between the CSS *Virginia* and the USS *Monitor* at the Battle of Hampton Roads in Virginia. The result was a draw, with no clear winner.

CSS VIRGINIA

4 INCHES
thickness of armor plating

263 FEET
length

10
guns

WATER
The Union Navy

3,000 MILES
length of the Union's initial plans for a naval blockade around the Confederacy, called the "Anaconda Plan"

40 ships in the Union navy in 1861

675 ships in the Union navy by 1865

$275,000 cost to build the *Monitor*

1ST rank in size by number of ships of the Union navy worldwide in 1865

360 DEGREES
rotation of turret

1 turret

USS MONITOR

2 11-inch guns

172 FEET
length

WOMEN AT WAR
BY THE 3s

30 minimum age of women serving as nurses in the Union

3,200 women who served as nurses in the Union

Women in the North and South participated in the war effort. They nursed wounded soldiers and fed troops. They also provided support to the armies stationed near their homes. Nursing and identifying missing soldiers were important tasks for Northern women. One nurse, Clara Barton, was able to identify tens of thousands of missing men using prisoner-of-war records and casualty lists. After the war, she went on to found the American Red Cross.

63,000

letters Clara Barton received from the families of Union soldiers searching for missing loved ones

CLARA BARTON

1873

year the first formal nursing school for women opened its doors, eight years after the end of the Civil War

3

years that Northern woman Jennie Hodgers served in the Union army. She pretended to be a man and went by the name Albert Cashier.

THE BLOODY BATTLES OF ANTIETAM AND GETTYSBURG

The Battle of Antietam

SEPTEMBER 17, 1862
date of the Battle of Antietam, the deadliest single-day battle in United States history

3,650
soldiers who died in the Battle of Antietam

5TH
rank in number of casualties in all Civil War battles

Casualties

10,316		
12,401		

| 0 | 5,000 | 10,000 |

▢ Confederate   ▢ Union

500 cannons involved in the battle

15 age of Union bugler Private Johnny Cook, who was awarded the Medal of Honor for his efforts to continue firing cannons after their operators had died

The Battle of Gettysburg

JULY 1–JULY 3, 1863
dates of the Battle of Gettysburg

1ST rank in number of casualties of all Civil War battles

Casualties

28,063	
23,049	

0   5,000   10,000   15,000   20,000   25,000

☐ Confederate   ☐ Union

3,000
horses that lost their lives at Gettysburg

10
roads leading into the town of Gettysburg, making it easy to move troops to and from the battle

SHERMAN'S MARCH
TO THE SEA

Union General William T. Sherman successfully attacked Atlanta, Georgia, in July 1864. Following this campaign, he hoped to press onward and destroy the South's resources in Georgia. He marched his troops from Atlanta to the coastal town of Savannah, Georgia, starting on November 15. Sherman destroyed railways, factories, and farmland along the way. His march to the sea was a major setback for the Confederacy.

36 days the march lasted
(from November 15–December 20, 1864)

2 routes Sherman used, dividing his army, to confuse the Confederate forces trying to prevent his march

10 railroads that Sherman's troops disabled by twisting rails and tearing up bridges

supplies Sherman **confiscated** on his march to the sea

15,000 cattle

500,000 pounds of bacon and pork

1 MILLION bushels of corn

3 MILLION pounds of flour and other grains

5,000 horses

3 major objectives for the march

✓ destroy manufacturing plants

✓ tear up railroads

✓ destroy farmland and farm equipment

confiscate—to seize or take

SURRENDER
AT APPOMATTOX

Union troops were deep into the South by early 1865. The Confederate forces were tired and short on food. General Lee attempted to fight his way toward supplies for his army, but Union forces surrounded him in Virginia. Following the Battle of Appomattox Court House, he had no choice but to surrender.

3 HOURS
time the initial battle lasted before Lee retreated with his army and surrendered

April 9, 1865
date of General Robert E. Lee's surrender to General Ulysses S. Grant at Appomattox Court House in Appomattox County, Virginia

25 MINUTES
duration of the meeting between the two generals

25,000

meals sent to the hungry Confederate troops by the Union army following the surrender

25,500

approximate number of Confederate troops Union General Grant **paroled** and sent home rather than taking prisoner

34

days between Lee's surrender and the last battle of the Civil War in Palmito Ranch, Texas. Some Confederate soldiers in Texas had refused to surrender, even after hearing about the end of the war.

parole—to release

27

AFTERMATH

Casualties

■ Battle Deaths   ▨ Deaths from Disease   ☐ Wounded

Union   642,427

Confederate   483,026

100,000   200,000   300,000   400,000   500,000   600,000   700,000

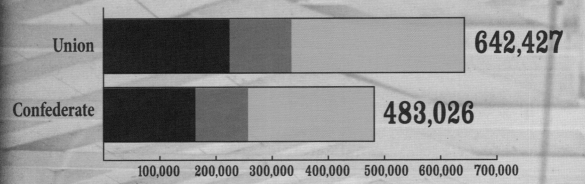

620,000   **644,000**

600,000

400,000

200,000

approximate number of American
deaths in the Civil War

approximate number of American
deaths in all other U.S. wars combined

Lincoln Assassinated

APRIL 14, 1865
date Lincoln was assassinated

1 bullet fired at Lincoln's head by the assassin, an actor and Southern sympathizer named John Wilkes Booth

3 words spoken by Booth after shooting Lincoln: "Sic semper tyrannis," meaning "Thus always to **tyrants**"

Reconstruction

13TH AMENDMENT
the law passed that officially abolished slavery; it took effect in December 1865

5
temporary military districts the Reconstruction Act of 1867 divided the South into

JULY 15, 1870
date that the last former Confederate state, Georgia, rejoined the United States

3,000
number of schools built in the South by the Freedmen's Bureau, a government agency that helped former slaves

150,000
number of African-American students who attended these schools

tyrant—a leader who is above the law and holds power through cruelty and violence

GLOSSARY

abolish (uh-BOL-ish)—to get rid of something completely

artilleryman (ar-TILL-er-ee-man)—a soldier who operates cannons or other large guns used during battles

casualty (KAZH-yuhl-tee)—a soldier who is dead, wounded, missing, or captured after a battle

confiscate (KAN-fis-KAYT)—to seize or take

enlisted (en-LIST-ed)—enrolled in the army or other branch of the military

flank (FLANK)—the side of a military formation

fortification (FORT-i-fi-KAY-shun)—a structure used to defend a city

fugitive (FYOO-juh-tiv)—a person who has escaped and is hiding from people who wish to capture or harm him or her

inauguration (in-AW-gyu-RAY-shun)—a ceremony to place a new president in office

mortar (MORE-tur)—a cannon that fires bombs at high angles and at short ranges

parole (pah-ROLL)—to release

secede (suh-SEED)—to leave a political group

siege (SEEJ)—the act of surrounding a city and its inhabitants in hopes of capturing it

skirmish (SKER-mish)—a minor fight between small groups of troops

tyrant (tie-RANT)—a leader who is above the law and holds power through cruelty and violence

READ MORE

Bearce, Stephanie. *Top Secret Files: The Civil War: Spies, Secret Missions, and Hidden Facts from the Civil War.* Waco, Tex.: Prufrock Press, 2014.

Fitzgerald, Stephanie. *The Split History of the Civil War.* North Mankato, Minn.: Compass Point Books, 2013.

Stanchak, John. *Civil War.* New York: DK Publishing, 2011.

CRITICAL THINKING USING THE COMMON CORE

1. What do the graphs on pages 8 and 11 show about workers in the Union and the Confederacy? Do you think the percentages could have provided an advantage for either side in war? Why or why not? (Integration of Knowledge and Ideas)

2. How do the graphs on page 28 help you understand how deadly the Civil War was? Why was it so deadly? Support your answer with information from the text and from at least two other online or print sources. (Integration of Knowledge and Ideas)

INTERNET SITES

FactHound offers a safe, fun way to find Internet sites related to this book. All of the sites on FactHound have been researched by our staff.

Visit *www.facthound.com*

Type in this code: 9781491442951

INDEX

TITLES IN THIS SET: